Thomas Willing Balch

**International Courts of Arbitration, 1874**

Thomas Willing Balch

**International Courts of Arbitration, 1874**

ISBN/EAN: 9783743310513

Manufactured in Europe, USA, Canada, Australia, Japa

Cover: Foto ©ninafisch / pixelio.de

Manufactured and distributed by brebook publishing software
(www.brebook.com)

Thomas Willing Balch

**International Courts of Arbitration, 1874**

# INTERNATIONAL

# COURTS OF ARBITRATION

BY

THOMAS BALCH

1874

REPRINTED AT PHILADELPHIA
ALLEN, LANE & SCOTT
1896

# PRELIMINARY NOTE.

This pamphlet was first published in *The Law Magazine and Review* (London) for November, 1874 (page 1026), and afterwards printed in this country. In the present reprint I have incorporated some changes in the phraseology that I found in the annotations in my father's own copy, on which he had written "author's copy"; I have added also notes 11 and 14, taken from the same source.

THOMAS WILLING BALCH.

PHILADELPHIA, February 22d, 1896.

# INTERNATIONAL
# COURTS OF ARBITRATION.

————————◄•►————————

TEN years ago the grave questions involved in the
escape of the *Alabama* and her subsequent depredations were the subject of much thought and anx-
iety, and many were the suggestions made by the
friends of peace as to a possible disposition of the controversy without resort to war. The situation had no
encouraging aspect. Indeed, it is difficult to realize
to-day how very hostile and angry were the two
parties. The attitude assumed throughout by the
English Government was such as to preclude appar-
ently any hope of adjustment, and the American
Minister at London was obliged to content himself
at last with merely sending in a fresh claim for
damages in a stereotyped phraseology. As the war
for secession approached its close the Americans be-
gan to realize somewhat the enormous losses attend-
ant upon it, not the least of which was the absolute

destruction of their commerce. The temper of the people was thoroughly roused, and any hostile demonstration at Washington would have met with a hearty and unanimous response throughout the country. President Lincoln not only remained calm himself, but wisely calmed, as far as he could, the popular excitement.

The most common method of settling national disputes, in modern times, where resort was had to arbitration, had been a reference to a monarch selected by the contending parties. But this plan was open to serious objections. Experience had disclosed that sovereigns were not free from the weaknesses of less exalted persons, and that prince and peasant alike, when once appointed sole arbiter, cannot resist man's innate tendency to find some award which will "split the difference," and which usually leaves the respective disputants equally dissatisfied. The United States had refused some years previously to accept such an award. A similar experience would have merely further exasperated a contest already sufficiently inflamed and imbittered.

Another objection was in the great difficulty of finding a reigning sovereign who would prove acceptable to both parties. Napoleon III. was of a restless, yet dreamy character. He was not a statesman, scarcely even a politician. He was not satisfied with mere political intrigue, for it was his nature to conspire. In 1859, therefore, obeying in part the behests of his temperament, he undoubtedly held guilty relations with some of the Southern gentlemen then in Paris, afterwards very prominent in the Confederate Councils. At the time, these relations were more or less matters of surmise or report. Later, they were stated in detail in the *Indépendance Belge*, in the winter of 1860–61, and were said to have been in substance, that an appeal had been made to the Emperor as head of the French race, on the ground that the larger part of the white inhabitants of Louisiana, of Florida, and South Carolina, and a portion of them in the other States, were of French extraction ; that thereupon had been promised to these self-constituted plenipotentiaries an immediate recognition by France and England of the Seceding States, in case the separation was peaceably effected, and a prompt recognition as belligerents in case of an armed struggle.[1] Some not very obscure intimations were given that at need something more than moral and political support might

---

[1] It has been recently stated in the newspapers that the Comte de Paris, in the forthcoming volumes of *La Guerre Civile en Amérique*, will demonstrate that the French and English proclamations to this effect were premature, and contrary to the recognized usages of amical nations.

be relied on. This remarkable communication was
doubtless no more than a correcter statement of the
reports of the day. At all events it passed unchal-
lenged, and subsequent events led close observers
to believe, that it had been prepared by some one
in authority. Not only was the Mexican expedition
undertaken, but the Emperor and his ministers were
actively at work, meddling, plotting against the
American Government, until at last they went so far
as to actually invite England and Russia to co-oper-
ate with France and insist upon an armistice.[2]

This mischievous activity was probably of more
service than otherwise to the Northern States; but
it had in one way or another provoked expressions of
opinion from such important personages as von Bis-
marck, von Beust, Gortschakoff, and others, that it
might be fairly said that there did not remain a court
which was not in some way so compromised that it
was quite impossible to find a royal referee.

---

[2] After these lines were sent to the printers, I received from a
friend a cutting from the *New York Express*, September 1st, giving an account of an interview between Prince Gortschakoff and
the American Minister at St. Petersburg, in which the Russian
Chancellor is represented as going even further than is stated
in the published Diplomatic Correspondence  The article asserts
that in the event of any European interference, the Czar would
have aided the Northern States with his fleet then at New York.

Another grave objection to asking a sovereign to act as arbitrator lay in the fact, that a decision in the case of the *Alabama* could not be arrived at without passing in review almost all that part of international law which related to neutrals. A very serious matter indeed, in which the whole world was interested; an occasion which ought to serve for a great and marked progress, and a settlement on a firmer and more just basis of the rules which should govern neutrals and belligerents. The United States had naturally, before their independence was recognized, and at all times subsequently, maintained that the evils of a war should fall on the belligerents alone. Neutrals had hardships enough to bear in the commercial disorders and the financial losses consequent upon a serious disturbance of the general peace; therefore, the only possible pretense for the interference of a belligerent with a neutral was that of self-defense; in other words, to prevent the neutral from giving "aid and comfort" to the enemy, and they contended that the sea-going vessels of a neutral were entitled to all the immunities and privileges of home waters. The American Government persistently endeavored by its diplomacy, by the decisions of its judicial tribunals, by resolutions in Congress, by declarations in the messages of its Presidents, to

have these just and righteous principles recognized.
In fact, it was for this that their last war with Great
Britain (1812–15) was fought. The United States,
it was supposed, would certainly press for an accep-
tation of these principles. But it was not likely that
England would ever consent to relinquish her own
long-cherished interpretation of the law of the sea.
"The coarse dialectics of the older English judges"[3]
had "mixed sovereign and belligerent powers;"[4] and,
inspired by the spirit and precedents of the semi-
barbarous times and deeds of Drake and Raleigh,
claimed the right to sit in judgment in its own tribunals, according to its own forms of procedure, upon
the acts, the rights, the property, and even the liber-
ties of citizens of a neutral state. From its courts,
no matter how flagrant the wrong done, there was no
appeal except a diplomatic representation to the king.
It is not surprising, therefore, that the claims of Eng-

[3] *Wharton's Criminal Law.* Preface to 7th ed., 1874 : xviii.
[4] *Belligerent and Sovereign Rights as regards Neutrals during the War of Secession* : Boston, 1873. This is the able and
learned argument of the Hon. William Beach Lawrence, in the
case of the *Circassian*, before the Commissioners appointed under
the twelfth article of the Treaty of Washington, and has much
professional weight from the fact that the International Tribunal
reversed the decision of the highest American Federal Court, as
reported in 2 Wallace's U. S. Supreme Court Reports, 135.

lish captors were upheld to the extremest limit possible, nor that many of the decisions of the English maritime tribunals were rank with injustice. Even when the increasing navies of other nations weighed sufficiently upon England's statesmen to obtain her assent to the declaration in the Treaty of Paris (April 16th, 1856), that an enemy's property on board neutral vessels, and neutral property found in an enemy's vessel, should be free from capture, except contraband of war, yet as, unfortunately, there was no formal definition of what should be considered contraband of war, British jurists forthwith applied their own narrow interpretation, and maintained that the products of a neutral state, though not directly applicable to warlike uses, but which might incidentally aid or assist a belligerent, were within the meaning of the phrase. It was not therefore probable that, if so much of the old leaven remained, there would be any chance of England consenting to appear before a sovereign and to submit to his award.

Those who strove and yearned for a peaceable solution of these grave questions neither abandoned hope nor allowed themselves to be disheartened. Mr. Cobden wrote to me from Midhurst, March 12th, 1865: "I have great faith in the aggregate intelligence of your country whenever its attention is

forced by adverse circumstances to a serious study
of politics. When the war is over you will have a
great financial difficulty to deal with. * * * But
you will soon surmount all these follies when the
nation finds itself in the school of adversity." These
words are the more noteworthy in that they were
written but a few days before his lamented death.

Other modes of adjustment were suggested and
discussed. Precedents were sought for and exam-
ined, and the research disclosed such various schemes,
almost stratagems, for settling disputes without re-
course to war, that one was tempted to assert that
a philosophy directly the reverse of that upheld by
the author of "Leviathan" was more in consonance
with the nature of man.[5] After mature reflection a
Court of Arbitration, in substance that developed in
the following letter, was proposed to various jurists
who took an interest in the matter.

In November, 1864, during a short visit to America, I had an opportunity of mentioning the proposed Court of Arbitration to President Lincoln.
He observed that the idea was a good one in the
abstract, but that in the then temper of the American people it was neither possible nor popular. In
fact, as he quaintly expressed it, we were not near

<hr/>

[5]*Libertas.* Molesworth's ed., 1839, ii., 157 *et seq.*

enough to the millennium for such methods of settling international quarrels.  Still, he thought the
"idea worth airing."

A draft outline of the proposed Court of Arbitration was refused by more than one editor; but
at last Mr. Greeley, who feared no unpopularity
where a cause was, as he thought, entitled to a
hearing, gave it a place in the columns of the *New
York Tribune*, March 18th, 1865.  The letter was addressed to the able and conscientious correspondent
of that journal at Paris, Mr. W. H. Huntington, and
was as follows:—

"PARIS, March 3d, 1865.

"MY DEAR SIR,—You asked me to put in writ-
ing the observations which I made to you yesterday
touching the outstanding questions between England
and the United States.  I should be sorry to make
you read all that you so kindly listened to.   It
would be to tax you rather too severely.  But the
current of my remarks was to this effect:

"I. That both England and the United States pre-
ferred claims which, if not judiciously managed, might
and perhaps would lead to war.

"II. That the American claims were chiefly the
depredations of the *Alabama*, whilst it seemed from

the tenor of Mr. Layard's recent speech, that the
British claims were also such as to rest upon questions of law. Neither set of claims was strictly national; they were rather those of individuals, mer-
chants, shipowners, and others.

"III. That as to such claims, war was a barbarous
manner of enforcing them; that the most successful
war would after all be a most expensive and unsat-
isfactory process of litigation; and that the civilized
and Christian way of ascertaining their validity and
extent should be by arbitration.

"IV. That the best manner of composing such a
Court of Arbitration would be, that each party should
select some competent jurist, those two to select an
umpire. The claims to be presented, proved and
argued before this Court, whose decisions should be
final and without appeal.

"V. That such a proposition, proceeding from our
Government, would, without doubt, receive the coun-
tenance and support of all intelligent Englishmen.
It is true that some of the speeches recently made
in Parliament about us and Canada are of a nature to
discourage such expectations. On the other hand, it
must be borne in mind that these gentlemen form
a class apart; that it is their political faith to believe
and say unseemly things of Republican institutions,

of the men, habits of life, and principles of action developed under them. But it was long ago that the wisest of men gave us the measure of such people, and the experience of mankind has confirmed his judgment.

"VI. Such a proposition from our Government would at once quiet all the foolish alarms which have, or appear to have, taken possession of so many persons in England. It would also uphold and strengthen all the advocates of progress. It would give greater force to their arguments in favor of just reforms and liberty; and this not only in Great Britain, but throughout Europe. The abandonment of the old system of arbitration by a reference to a Sovereign, more or less unfit from the very nature of his position, and the introduction of a tribunal, almost republican in its character, whose decisions would have a weight as precedents, an authority heretofore unknown as expositions of international law, would be no trifling events in the march of Democratic Freedom.

"VII. Such a proposition would also be in accord with our traditional policy of peace and goodwill towards men.

"The most serious objection that has been urged, so far as I have heard, against such a Court of

Arbitration, is the difficulty of finding gentlemen not already biased by their feelings or in some way committed in their opinions.

"This objection applies, however, in a measure, to all human tribunals; it would apply to arbitration by a sovereign, and would leave us no solution other than the dread arbitrament of war. For myself, I cannot believe that there are not to be had in England and America gentlemen of the requisite learning, experience, and impartiality for a position so dignified and useful. At all events, there are many eminent men in Europe in every way qualified for this high duty. I have in my mind's eye a Swiss publicist,[6] who, after having filled the most responsible stations at home, is now worthily representing his people in their most important diplomatic post. The decisions rendered by him and gentlemen like him would be such as two great and free nations could accept with satisfaction. I dare say he has friendly feelings towards the Republic, but he cannot be wanting in like sentiments for the old Champion of Liberty. The preferences of such enlightened statesmen could not possibly be of a character to

---

[6] I may now say that this referred to that most worthy, high-minded gentleman, Dr. Kern, formerly President of the Federal Council, but then Minister to France.

influence their judgments, and the parties most interested might well be content to abide their award.

"Believe me, my dear sir, yours sincerely,

"THOMAS BALCH."

The publication of this letter proved very conclusively, that whatever might be the merits of the proposed Court of Arbitration, it certainly was not popular in the United States. Two years later the accomplished editor of *Social Science*, Mr. Westlake, was induced by an English jurist,[7] for whose opinion he had great respect, to reprint it in that periodical, March 15th, 1867, and spoke of it as an "important letter," but made no further comment. Nevertheless, the idea was well received by such men as Laboulaye, Henri Moreau, and other members of the *Societé de la Législation Comparée*, in France ; by von Holtzendorff, Kapp, and other honored publicists in Germany. That the letter in which the plan was originally sketched out should be lost sight of was quite natural and usual. I know of no more affecting picture of the *sic vos, non vobis*, haps and mishaps of literary life than that traced by Blüntschli in his introduction to his " Code of Belligerent Laws,"[8]

---

[7] [Professor James Lorimer.—T. W. B.]

[8] *Le Droit International Codifié*, par M. Blüntschli, translated by M. Lardy, Secretary to the Swiss Legation, Paris, 1870.

where he tells how the men who propounded or elaborated some great governing principle of International Law have, in the course of time, been as absolutely forgotten as the skillful but obscure workman who converts the dingy pebble into the brilliant gem. The proposed tribunal was, however, made the subject of some articles and two or three prelections. Discussion gave it vitality. It grew in favor, was considered plausible, then feasible, and finally took a visible form and shape in the Treaty of Washington.

It is not within the purview of these observations to discuss at large the provisions of that Treaty. The Three Rules are so obnoxious to numerous and serious objections that it is much to be hoped in the interest of neutrals and honest people generally, that the United States and England will disagree so permanently and effectually as to their construction and meaning as to have nothing more said or heard of them, except the just and severe criticism and condemnation which they will probably receive from the distinguished jurists who are soon to meet in Geneva. Had the synod of diplomatists who framed these obscurely expressed rules profited by the occasion to overthrow some of the barbarisms still upheld, and, for example, joined in adopting as a principle of law the decision of the Supreme Court at Berlin, "that every contract for introducing contraband goods into a friendly State is contrary to law and morals,"[9] they would have rendered a vast service to mankind.    Perhaps, also, had Mr. Cobden lived, his counsels might have so far prevailed as to have given to the Treaty as a whole a character and spirit which would have rendered it more acceptable to the English people at large, more auspicious also for the future of peaceable arbitraments of international difficulties.    It is not to be overlooked that from time to time ebullitions, both in and out of Parliament, such as the question of Sir Henry Wolfe, the observations of Earl Russell, prove that there still exists a certain uneasiness as to the present as well as the past position of Great Britain in that transaction.    A few lines from one of his later letters exhibit the standpoint from which Mr. Cobden regarded the conduct of his own country, and from it we may infer the character which he would have probably endeavored to impress upon the negotiations:—

"MIDHURST, 3d January, 1865.

"MY DEAR MR. BALCH,—I was very sorry to miss the opportunity of seeing you in London.    There are

---

[9] *Heffter*, cited by Lawrence, Com. iii., 401.

very many topics on which I should liked to have talked with you. I think it depends entirely on the discretion of your own authorities at Washington to remain at peace with all the world until your civil war is ended. I do not say that you have not grievances; but one quarrel at a time, as Mr. Lincoln says, is enough for a nation or an individual.[10] *With the British Government I do not think, on the whole, you have as much to be angry about as to be grateful for what it has refused to do."*

Those Americans, who remember the official account given in the *Moniteur* of the visit of Messrs. Osborne and Lindsay to Compiègne, or recall the letters exchanged between M. Thouvenel and Mr. Dayton, or the avowed purposes of the Mexican expedition, will probably concur in the opinion thus expressed by Mr. Cobden.

Whatever the criticisms to which the Treaty may in whole or in parts be open, there remained for the friends of peace and international arbitration the great, triumphant fact that the Court did meet at Geneva and by its award averted, as far as human

---

[10] An observation which Mr. Lincoln made to the writer in the conversation above mentioned. [See page 8.—T. W. B.]

probabilities go, an appeal to arms.   That the United
States and English Commissioners were rather too
national and demonstrative, does not seriously mili-
tate against such courts, but merely touches the construction of them ; and we have a notable proof of
their value and integrity in the Court of the Mixed
Commission which sat at Newport in 1873, to hear
and decide upon the English and American claims.
In the case of the *Circassian*, already mentioned,
Count Corti, the President of the Commission, took it
upon himself to overrule the decision of the Supreme
Court of the United States, an act of high judicial
courage, which, apart from its legal bearings, is an
omen of great promise, for it proves that men of
character will sit in such dignified tribunals and
render impartial decisions.[11]

Likewise that the United States has kept the money
so promptly and honorably paid does not touch the
question of international arbitration or its desirable-
ness.   The prolonged struggle in Congress over the
disposition of these funds may be never so dishonest

---

[11] Count Corti tells me that his reason for cutting down the
claim was this : That it is true the blockade was raised by Federal
success ; but such was not the case when the *Circassian* sailed.
She, therefore, left *in delicto*, and continued so, till nearly the end
of her voyage.

or discreditable to the American legislative authorities, but it does not impugn the justice of the decision by which they were placed in the hands of that
Government in its capacity as a great national trus-
tee.   To present the claims for "indirect losses" may
have been an act of audacious chicane which reflected
no credit on those who did it; but the tribunal did
itself honor, and gave us a valuable precedent by
ruling against their admissibility.

The friends of International Courts of Arbitration
may fairly assert that this mode of settling great
national questions has been fully and successfully
tried, that it may be considered as having thereby
passed into and henceforth forming a distinct part
of that uncertain and shapeless mass of decision
and dicta which we call International Law.   Without
participating in the visions so grandly developed by
Zuinglius,[12] and so fondly cherished by Grotius, of
the good time, a good time to be won only by toil
and unremitting efforts,—

"When the war-drums throbbed no longer, and the battle flags
    were furl'd,
In the Parliament of man, in the Federation of the World,"[13]

we may reasonably expect that through such tribunals, through their proceedings and decisions, and not

---

[12] *Civitas Christiana.*      [13] Tennyson.

through empirical codes, we may ultimately arrive at some more tangible and better ordered system of International Law ; one to which the assent of civilized peoples may be given greatly to the benefit of mankind.

A deep, well-settled conviction that this great advance in human progress is not only imminent, but has already commenced and is assured for the future, makes it incumbent on its advocates to examine carefully and philosophically the various forms in which Courts of Arbitration may be organized, and especially the limits within which their authority may be beneficially exercised. I received not very long since a communication from Professor Lorimer, notable for its calm and magisterial discussion of these points. As the *New York Tribune* had given light and life to my original letter, it seemed but proper that the observations of this distinguished jurist should appear first in its columns. They were accompanied April 11th, 1874, by an article supposed to be from the pen of the chief editor, Mr. Whitelaw Reid, the character and interest of which induce me to reprint it here instead of any introductory remarks of my own.

## "LIMITS OF ARBITRATION.

"About nine years ago, the *Tribune* published a letter from Mr. Thomas Balch, recommending almost precisely the plan of arbitration in the *Alabama* case, which after infinite discussion, was finally adopted and carried out to so satisfactory a conclusion at Geneva. It is in reference to that early communication of Mr. Balch that Prof. James Lorimer, the Regius Professor of Public Law and of the Law of Nations, in the University of Edinburgh, has written to him the letter which we print this morning. It is worthy of special attention as the mature utterance of a publicist who, having devoted his life to the study of international law and the theories of international relations, and having been a prominent advocate of arbitration and a constant protestant against the barbarism of war, retains enough of impartial calmness of judgment to recognize the limits which are probably imposed upon the capabilities of arbitration by the conditions of human nature and civilized policy.

"Professor Lorimer expects nothing of arbitration, for instance, in cases where one party is morally incapable of entering rationally into a contract, or physically incapable of enforcing its provisions when made. This excludes most of the fighting which ordinarily falls to the lot of England. It is evident that neither the Emperor Theodore nor the King Coffee-Kalkalli was capable of appreciating any procedure except the one which was put in force against them both.

Neither is there any prospect that the civilized world will ever be able to interfere with the progress or the result of civil wars. Prof. Lorimer does not state that as his own conclusion, but his references to the Paris Commune and our own war of the Rebellion would lead in that direction. In cases where the real object of a war is to determine the relative strength of two nations, and where an unquestioned supremacy is to be the prize of victory, it is clear that arbitration is hopeless, except by an armed intervention of allied powers too imposing to be resisted. It was, for example, impossible to prevent the Franco-Prussian conflict. The trivial question of the interview of Benedetti and King William in the garden at Ems, might of course have been arranged in any half-hour's session of a jury of gentlemen. But the genuine, unmanageable question which remained behind, was the one which could not be peacefully settled; that is, whether Prussia or France was the stronger. The field of arbitration seems therefore to be limited to the class of disputes of which the *Alabama* and the San Juan Boundary questions are specimens. How narrow this field is, may be seen when we reflect that except in case of great popular excitement they would never have been made a pretext for war, and that if this excitement had really existed they could not have been referred to arbitration. The world is yet far from that millennial condition when reason and charity are to exercise a commanding influence upon disputes between nations. The better sense of mankind has come, however, to recognize the irrational character of war, and the advocates of peaceful international tribunals are probably not too sanguine in hoping that the future is theirs. But at present their nearest attainable ideal is the establishment of an international organization of force which shall prevent wars by armed menace. There are many who doubt whether armies will not survive courts of justice, and Mr. Lorimer cogently observes: 'When I hear of a State of which the citizens have become so reasonable and dispassionate as to abolish compulsory jurisdiction and to trust to voluntary arbitration, I shall then begin to have higher hopes of international reason and moderation, and, consequently, of international arbitration.'"

The letter from Professor Lorimer, thus spoken of, was as follows:—

"No. 1, BRUNTSFIELD CRESCENT, EDINBURGH,
"FEBRUARY 10th, 1874.

"Considering the interest which is everywhere taken in International Arbitration at present, and more especially with a view to the discussion that will take place at the meeting of the International Institute at Geneva in October, I think it very desirable that you should republish the letter which you addressed to the 'New York Tribune' in 1865, adding to it such suggestions as your observation of subsequent events may enable you to offer.

"I do not know to what extent that letter, or anything else you said or did, may have led to the negotiation of the Treaty of Washington, by which the threatened war between our countries is believed by many to have been averted; but certain it is, that the letter was a very remarkable anticipation of the treaty which was negotiated six years afterward. The tribunal which you suggested almost exactly corresponded to that appointed under Article XII. of the Treaty, and even the great tribunal which sat at Geneva under Article I. was only a fuller realization of your original conception, by a larger infusion of the neutral element than you had contemplated, into the Court. In this respect it certainly was an improvement. But for the presence of the neutral judges it is doubtful if the work would have been brought to a successful issue, and I think it very worthy of consideration whether, on all future occasions, the Commissioners ought not to be appointed exclusively from neutrals.

"In his introduction to his pamphlet on *Belligerent and Sovereign Rights*, which contains his very able pleading in the case of the *Circassian*, Mr. W. Beach Lawrence remarks on the want of judicial dignity and impartiality displayed by the Commissioners of both the interested nations, and adds: 'In that tribunal there were three other members, and two of them might, perhaps, without serious inconvenience, have been withdrawn from the bench.' I confess I am much disposed to agree with him. The judges of such a court, as it seems to me, ought all to be neutrals, the belligerents, so to speak, appearing only in their true character as litigants. Whether their judges ought all to be chosen by neutrals is another question. With a view to removing or mitigating the aversion which proud and jealous nations naturally feel to intrusting their honor and their interests to others, it might probably be expedient that each litigant should retain the direct appointment of one member of the court, binding itself not to select him from its own citizens, or from the citizens of any State that was dependent upon it.

"But the chief difficulties attending International Arbitration have reference, not to the organization of suitable tribunals, but to the determination of the character of the parties capable of organizing them, and the character of the questions that can be submitted to them.   In this country there is a tendency to pooh-pooh arbitration altogether, on the ground of the limited sphere of its possible operation; and to save it from ridicule and vindicate for it the position to which it is really entitled, I do think it very important that we jurists should try whether we cannot eliminate the impossible cases and moderate the expectations of its injudicious advocates.   It is very much this task which the Institute proposes to itself in the first instance, and I know no one more able to aid in its accomplishment than yourself, privileged as you are to enjoy the society of such jurists as Mr. Lawrence.   As I belong to the committee which the Institute has appointed to study the kindred subject of 'The Three Rules,' I shall not be called upon to express my opinion on this subject previous to the meeting, and I shall therefore mention to you now, in a very few words, what has occurred to me :—

"*First:* Arbitration being a contract by which the parties agree to abide by the decision of a third, is possible only between two parties, both of whom possess rational, and, as such, contracting will.   This cuts off arbitration between civilized nations and barbarians, because barbarians are incapable of entering into such a contract. Civilized nations could not trust to the decision of the arbitrators whom barbarians might appoint; and even supposing them to appoint civilized men, civilized nations could not trust to their acceptance of the decision in which their own arbitrators had concurred. If the conduct of civilized nations to barbarians be unjust, it is a form of injustice which may be prevented—as in the case of the slave trade—by the condemnation and even by the intervention of other civilized nations; but it cannot be prevented by arbitration.

"*Second:* There are internal as well as external barbarians to whom these observations apply. Arbitration between the Commune of Paris, for example, and the Government of Versailles, would have been as much out of place as between us and the Ashantees, or between a criminal and the public prosecutor.

"*Third:* Arbitration is inapplicable where the question at issue has reference to the relative value of States—where it is asked, for example, whether their historical position in relation to each other is or is not now their true position. So far as the Franco-German war was a fight for the hegemony of continental Europe, it did not admit of arbitration, for the very obvious reason that that was a question which, if it must be decided, could be decided only by trial of strength. On the other hand, in so far as the Franco-German war arose from the question whether France was entitled to the boundary of the Rhine, on geographical grounds, or whether Germany was entitled to Alsace and Lorraine on historical and ethnological grounds, it was a fit subject for arbitration, however difficult it might have been to induce either power to think so. It would, I believe, have been physically possible for Russia, England, America, and Austria combined, to have forced their services as mediators even upon two such formidable combatants as France and Germany, and perhaps they might now prevent the too probable recurrence of war. But even in the most improbable and inconceivable event of their arbitration being accepted, by no decree arbitral could they have produced the facts that resulted from the late war, or could they now anticipate those which may result from another. Arbitration, like judicial action in any other form, can only declare a relation which already exists, whereas war brings about new relations, or at least converts those which existed *in posse* into relations *in esse*. On this ground I fear the Eastern Question too is beyond the reach of arbitration, that question, in its essence, being the question as to whether or not Russia be in reality the

preponderating power, and, as such, entitled to give
the law to the East of Europe and the West of Asia.
Here, however, there is one element favorable to
arbitration which did not exist in the case of France
and Germany, namely, the willingness of one of the
parties, at least (Turkey), to place herself unreserv-
edly into the hands of neutrals. I refrain altogether
from offering an opinion as to whether arbitration
was, at any time, possible in the relations between
the Northern and Southern States, previous to, or
during the course of your own great civil war, that
being a subject on which you are so much more able
to form an opinion than I am.

"These three cases, or classes of cases, then, are
the only ones I can think of at present that seem to
forbid the hope of ever being dealt with by arbitration. They leap over all the ordinary disputes
and disagreements of nations, which admit of being
measured by pecuniary compensation, or arranged
by the exchange or cession of territory, with a
view to the rectification of boundary lines and the
like. Even within these limits the action of courts
composed of neutral arbiters may be extremely useful in removing more speedily and with less irritation
than was possible by the arbitration of sovereigns or
by ordinary diplomacy, causes which interrupted inter-

national cordiality, and in the end may have led to
wars.   But it is not out of questions such as these
that great wars have generally arisen.   I doubt
whether you could mention a single war of any im-
portance between two civilized nations that arose sub-
stantially out of such a question as the *Alabama*
claims; and that question, too, would, in my opinion,
have been settled without war even although it had
not been settled by arbitration.[14]   It is well that we
have been spared the estrangement to which a trou-
blesome course of negotiation, probably extending
over years, must inevitably have led, and that we
have escaped the still more fatal consequences in
which such estrangement might have resulted.   But
it is well, too, that we should remember that, in our
international just as in our municipal relations, arbitration being voluntary on both sides, must always be
of the nature of a friendly suit; and that the first condition of its possibility is that one of the parties at all
events shall have previously come to the conclusion
that the question in dispute is not worth a war.   In this
case I suspect that a conclusion had been arrived at by
both parties, and hence the success of the arbitration.

---

[14] It was, more likely, because the questions to be adjudicated
came within the domain of "le Droit International *privé*" and
not "*public.*"

"Those who expect arbitration to become applicable to the graver disputes of nations are probably misled by the frivolous pretexts on which declarations of war are often made at the last—such, for example, as the Emperor not wishing to talk politics when he was drinking his waters, or after he had drunk them. But these are not the causes of war; deeper causes at least lie behind them, for which deeper remedies than arbitration must be found. We may hope that wars will diminish in frequency by the gradual action of a growing national reason, and the adoption of sounder political principles, national and international, till at last, like duelling in this country, they cease altogether. But if they are to be averted directly, I am convinced that that can be done only by the help of some form of international organization which shall render it possible to bring the armed intervention of neutral nations to bear on them. I fear you will think me a pessimist in this matter. I know that such is the opinion of many of my sanguine friends in Europe, and even of some of my colleagues of the Institute. But I cannot affect a confidence which I do not feel; and I am wholly unable to discover grounds for expecting results from arbitration in international relations which it does not yield in municipal relations, and this more especially when I reflect how far municipal organization has advanced beyond international organization, and municipal law beyond international law. When I hear of a State of which the citizens have become so reasonable and dispassionate as to abolish compulsory jurisdiction and to trust to voluntary arbitration, I shall then begin to have higher hopes of international reason and moderation, and consequently of International Arbitration. I do not say that an international legislature, an international judicature, and an international executive, after the manner I have elsewhere suggested, are aspirations capable of realization. Perhaps, as M. Rolin-Jacquemyns[15] maintains, they are remedies which might prove more dreadful than even the terrible malady they were intended to cure. But I do say that they are the only direct remedies for war, and that, apart from them, we must be contented to teach, to wait, and—to pray.

"Believe me, etc.,

"J. LORIMER."[16]

---

[15] Editor of *La Revue du Droit International.*

[16] Professor Lorimer is best known on this side of the Atlantic by his treatise, *The Institutes of Law as determined by the Principles of Nature*, Edinburgh, 1872 ; but his *Constitutionalism of the Future* and his *Political Progress not necessarily Democratic*, are well worthy the consideration of American publicists.

The foregoing remarks require no comment further than to express my hearty concurrence with nearly all of them. One point admits of an observation.

As to arbitration between the Northern and Southern States before the breaking out of the civil war in America:—

(*i.*) The Constitution of the United States was framed expressly with a view to avoid and prevent any sort of hostile dispute between the constituent members of the Union. It is beyond the purposes of this pamphlet to enter into an elaborate examination of the functions and powers of the Supreme Court, or the complex, delicate machinery of co-ordinate executive, legislative, and judicial powers, by which it was thought that all questions, how grave soever, would be peaceably and satisfactorily solved. Without attempting to cite Kent or Story, or other learned jurists, it is quite sufficient, in order to show that it was so understood at the time, to refer to the debates in the Virginia Convention prior to the adoption of the Federal Constitution, and especially to the adverse arguments of George Mason and the replies of James Madison.

(*ii.*) An extra-constitutional body or Peace Conference was in fact convened in Washington, composed of representatives from the different States. That its efforts proved abortive, and that the constitutional remedies for the alleged wrong of the South were not resorted to, were simply owing to the fact, that from the first, it was intended by the leading Southern politicians to disregard them and reject all attempts at settlement.  Both kinds of arbitration, that legally organized and prepared in advance, that which was advisory and voluntary, were summarily spurned, and there remained no other tribunal than that of force.

There are also other "signs of the times" which justify the advocates of International Arbitration in entertaining great hope for the future.  Railways, ocean steamers, telegraphs and newspapers, have created a solidarity amongst nations, such as has not heretofore existed, too occult as yet for its force to be fully appreciated, but whose influences are visible like the early streaks of the dawn.  Evangelical alliances, international meetings for scientific purposes, congresses to consider the treatment of criminals, the international law associations which are soon to assemble in Geneva, and various other societies, testify to the growth of this feeling.  The

advanced education of the working classes has provoked and fostered a spirit of inquiry amongst them,
and they too have their international gatherings,
where, amongst other things, they ask why wars in
which they are slaughtered by thousands should be
wantonly undertaken?[17]   The Congress lately convened at Brussels may be referred to as an evi-
dence that governments also commence to recognize
this tendency towards community amongst nations.
It is true that the United States were not represented, that England and France sent delegates
fettered by instructions, that Austria sent memo-
randa from her war department as well as from her
foreign office, and that other powers maintained a
guarded reserve.   The conferences of that Congress
may prove sterile from many causes, not the least of
which are the difficulties inherent in the very nature of
the subjects which they propose to regulate by codes.
*La Societé Française des amis de la Paix,*[18] protested
with great severity against articles III. and IV., as
"awakening indignation and horror in the breast of
every honest man."   The course of the Swiss, Span-

---

[17] "Pourquoi nous égorger?   Ne vaut-il pas mieux aimer?
Les peuples sont des frères."

[18] *Courier des Etats-Unis*, August 11th, 1874.   "Un Con-
grés de Dissidents."

ish, Dutch, Austrian, Swedish, and Belgian delegates during the debates clearly evinces the doubtful practicability of giving those articles an efficient or satisfactory action, should they be ever accepted. The outcry of the French as to the conduct of the Germans at Weissembourg, at Bazincourt, at Ablis, at Étrépagny and other places was loud at the time and has never ceased.[19] The Germans responded by solemn declarations that the so-called victims were individual adventurers, unorganized forces, and in these or in other ways amenable to the utmost rigors of the laws of war. In the matter of requisitions, the German history of the Franco-German war, prepared with the most elaborate care by the Prussian staff,[20] asserts that all the pains possible were taken to carry out in an orderly manner the proclamation of the King (August 8th), yet such were the obstacles, so serious the embarrassments, so numerous the infractions, that "it required the most energetic intervention of the superior officers to prevent disorder from spreading like a contagion"—an

---

[19] The latest French history of the war of 1870–71, by A. Wachter, Paris, 1874, has at page 152 a large wood cut, entitled "Massacre des blessés dans des fermes converties en ambulances. Épisode de Wissembourg."

[20] *La Guerre Franco-Allemande de 1870–71.*—Translation of Major Costa de Serda, Berlin, 1873–4, i., 422, 423.

experience not peculiar to that war, as may be seen from the nature and incidents of some of the claims presented to, and passed upon by, the Mixed Commission already referred to as organized under the Treaty of Washington. Much practical good can scarcely be expected therefore from the deliberation of the Congress touching such subjects. It furnishes, nevertheless, an element of hope in that the world has beheld a body of authorized delegates who have discussed in a common tongue some momentous questions, and cited Puffendorf, Vattel, Ortolan, and other authorities in support of their views. But above all, it is a proof that Governments as well as Peoples recognize the idea of a common humanity, that this idea exhibits vitality and an aggressive strength, that it exacts respect from the former, and will sooner or later respond to the aspirations and satisfy the needs of the latter.

NEWPORT, RHODE ISLAND, September 8th, 1874.

# APPENDIX.

[The following article was part of a letter written at Paris on October the 31st, 1874, to the Philadelphia *North American and United States Gazette*, and published in that paper on November the 14th. I am inclined to think that the author was Mr. W. H. Huntington (see page 9), for many years the Paris correspondent of the *New York Tribune.*—T. W. B.]

" The pamphlet of your fellow-townsman, Mr. Thomas Balch, on 'International Courts of Arbitration,' dated from Newport, Rhode Island, and for a copy of which I have to thank the author, has attracted much and deserved attention here, both from his own countrymen and others. In the first place, the pamphlet is acknowledged to be only a fair indication of the author's claims to be considered, in the words of the article quoted by him from the *New York Tribune* of April last, as 'the original recommender of almost precisely the plan of arbitration in the *Alabama* case, which was finally adopted and carried out to a conclusion at Geneva ;' or in the still more forcible language of his learned correspondent, Professor Lorimer, of Edinburgh, as 'the very remarkable anticipator (by his letter of March, 1865, that is addressed to the above-named journal) of the Treaty which was negotiated six years afterwards.' Such testimony paid to the real service rendered by Mr. Balch, both to his own country and the world at large, though coming late, must be extremely welcome, and will certainly take by surprise not a few even of those who may have hitherto thought themselves most fully acquainted with all the circumstances of that long controversy. At least such has been the impression left by its pages upon many here, both American and French, whose attention I have drawn to Mr. Balch's publication.

"But the pamphlet will be useful, and I am sure its author will be glad to think and intended that it should be so in other respects, as well as vindicating his own just rights and merits. Its excellent tone will tend, I trust, to clear any dregs of bitterness which may still cloud the good feelings which ought to exist between the kindred nations—nations who ought to understand more and more, since late events and in the present chaotic state of Europe, that they are the only two peoples between whom something far nearer and closer than any mere political alliance is possible, an alliance that is based on social, religious, family, literary, historical and a thousand other mutual associations, and all whose public and private institutions, however they may seem to differ occasionally in form, are in reality akin, and wear and ever must wear a strong family resemblance.    And with this view I am glad to see that Mr. Balch quotes the words of Mr. Cobden, to the effect that, while admitting grievances, America had 'more cause, on the whole, to be grateful to the British Government for what it refused to do, than angry with it for what it did,' or, he might have added, sometimes neglected to do.    I heard nearly the same sentiment from the lips of the lamented Mr. Dayton here in Paris, at the very crisis of the war; and none knew or were made to feel more deeply or painfully than he what the British Government had 'refused to do,' and by whom it had been asked so to do.    It is essential that the American people should understand that the attempts to injure them in England proceeded only from a party and a clique (such as will exist in all countries under similar circumstances), and not from the country itself at large, or its government; just as Mr. Balch so truly says, that the abuses uttered against America in the British Parliament proceeded from 'gentlemen who form a class apart' and 'whose political creed is to believe and say unseemly things of republican institutions.' But no man in his senses can now believe that such are the feelings of the British nation in general.

"But, above all, Mr. Balch's publication is valuable as keeping still before the world, at a moment when 'nation is literally rising against nation,' and when universal and obligatory personal service in France is being met by counter demonstrations of the *landsturm* in Germany, of keeping before the eyes of the world the fact that 'this mode of settling disputes has been fully and successfully tried' by two of the not least powerful and warlike nationalities of the world. It is useful also as freeing the movement in favor of arbitration from the merely Utopian and extravagant ideas of the peacemakers, the champions of *la paix à tout prix*, which serve only (as they did in 1849-50, with Victor Hugo at their head) to turn the whole thing into ridicule.

\*　　\*　　\*　　\*　　\*　　\*　　\*

" Professor Lorimer's letter of February last and Mr. Balch's comment upon it, show, not that wars can ever become impossible, but how far and where arbitration may be rendered always possible. And in doing this both writers confer a just boon upon their own generation and on posterity."

www.ingramcontent.com/pod-product-compliance
Lightning Source LLC
Chambersburg PA
CBHW032133080426
42733CB00008B/1054